CONTENTS

BunsOut.net

BunsOut.net Travel Guide is the travel guide for BunsOut.net: The Official Travel Guide and Community for Men Who Enjoy Naturism. The membership based website includes the travel guide, member profiles, groups and a newsfeed for information and photos sharing, a directory of nudist organizations, and other features. The website is updated and added to on a daily basis.
The separate travel guide, the e-book and printed book, are updated annually.

The travel guide is categorized by region. Within each region there are three categories:

LODGING: this section includes male-only clothing-optional resorts, hotels, motels, guesthouses, campsites, and RV parks. There are a few lodging places that are not male-only; they cater to the LGBTQ+ community and have been included because of their isolated location and lack of naturist options in that area.

OUTDOORS: this section includes clothing-optional beaches, lakes, rivers, hot springs, and other outdoor places to be nude. The locations are official and unofficial nude destinations.

WELLNESS: this section include clothing-optional yoga studios, gyms, saunas, spas, and retreat centers that cater to a male clientele. Some locations have female sections.

Some regions do not have all three categories, but all known clothing-optional places are listed.

Remember, things change. The clothing-optional places listed in the BunsOut,net Travel Guide are, to the best of our knowledge, still available to nudist. The website is updates daily, and the book will be updated annually. Please do your research in the meantime to make sure the listed places are correct and still available. Also, check local laws before partaking in nudist and clothing-optional activities.

If you know of a place that is not listed or if a location is no longer available, email us at bunsoutnet@gmail.com.

AFRICA

CANARY ISLANDS (SPAIN)

LODGING:

Atlantic Sun Beach
Playa del Inglés, Gran Carnia
https://mowhotels.com/es/atlantic-sun-beach.html

Birdcage Resort
Playa del Ingles, Las Palmas, Gran Carnia
https://birdcage-resort.amenitiz.io/en

Club Torso
Maspalomas, Las Palmas, Gran Carnia
https://www.clubtorso.com/en/p/resort

Seven
Maspalomas, Gran Carnia
https://mowhotels.com/es/seven-hotel-wellness.html

Vista Bonita
Maspalomas, Gran Carnia
https://mowhotels.com/en/vista-bonita-resort.html

OUTDOORS:

<u>Fuertaventura</u>

El Cofete Beach
Pájara
https://www.worldbeachguide.com/spain/el-cofete-beach.htm

Playa de Esquinzo (Butihondo)
El Cotillo
https://www.worldbeachguide.com/spain/playa-de-esquinzo.htm

Playa del Águila (La Escaleras)
El Cotillo
https://www.worldbeachguide.com/spain/playa-aguila.htm

Playa del Matorral (Morro Jable)
Pájara
https://www.worldbeachguide.com/spain/playa-del-matorral.htm

Sotavento Beach
Pájara
https://www.worldbeachguide.com/spain/sotavento.htm

Gran Carnaria

Maspalomas Sand Dunes & Gay Beach - Kiosk 7
Las Palmas
https://sites.google.com/flywebmakers.com/dunas-de-maspalomas/home

Playa Nudista Montaña Arena
Las Palmas
https://localguidegrancanaria.com/playa-montana-arena/

Playa del Confítal
Las Palms
https://www.worldbeachguide.com/spain/playa-del-confital.htm

Naked Boat
https://awayevents.es/naked-boat/

La Gomera

Playa del Inglés

Alajeró
https://www.worldbeachguide.com/spain/playa-del-ingles.htm

Lanzarote

Playa de la Cantería
Haría
https://www.worldbeachguide.com/spain/playa-de-la-canteria.htm

Playa de Las Conchas
Haría
https://www.worldbeachguide.com/spain/playa-de-las-conchas.htm

Playa Famara
Hária
https://www.worldbeachguide.com/spain/playa-famara.htm

Tenerife

Playa de Benijo
Santa Cruz de Tenerife
https://www.worldbeachguide.com/spain/playa-de-benijo.htm

Playa de las Gaviotas
Santa Cruz de Tenerife
https://www.worldbeachguide.com/spain/playa-de-las-gaviotas.htm

Playa de la Tejita
San Miguel
https://www.worldbeachguide.com/spain/playa-de-la-tejita.htm

Playa la Pelada
Arenas del Mar, Tenerife
https://beachsearcher.com/en/beach/724251167/playa-la-pelada

SOUTH AFRICA

LODGING:

VoëlkopGay Men's Guest Farm
Makolokwe / Johannesburg
https://voelkop.jimdofree.com

Pink Rose Guesthouse
Somerset West / Cape Town
https://www.pinkroseguesthouse.com/en/contact.php

OUTDOORS:

Sandy Beach
Cape Town
http://www.capetown.dj/beaches/SandyBay/SandyBay.htm

Lighthouse Beach
Port Alfred
http://www.naturistdirectory.com/South-Africa/1391/Port-Alfred-Beach

Umhlanga Lagoon
Durban
http://www.naturistdirectory.com/South-Africa/1392/Umhlanga-Beach

Secrets Beach
Port Elizabeth
https://beachsearcher.com/en/beach/710201132/secrets-beach

WELLNESS:

Brave Brothers
Cape Town
https://www.bravebrothers.co.za/

ASIA

CAMBODIA

LODGING:

Arthur & Paul
Phnom Penh
https://www.arthurandpaul.com/

Men's Resort & Spa
Reap Angkor
http://www.mens-resort.com/index.php

OUTDOORS:

Koh Rong Samloem Island
(off the coast of Sihanoukville)
https://www.tripsavvy.com/best-beaches-in-cambodia-5212842

JAPAN

OUTDOORS:

Chiba Beach
Chiba
(near Namihana station, just north of Onjuku)
https://jaredinnakano.wordpress.com/2013/07/13/gay-beach-in-chiba-offers-nudity-and-fraternity/

WELLNESS:

24 Kaikan (3 locations)
Tokyo
- Shinjuku-2-13-1 Shinjukuku
- Asakusa 2-29-16 Taitoku,
- KITA-UENO-1-8-7 Taitoku,
http://www.juno.dti.ne.jp/~kazuo24/english/english.htm

Jin-ya
Tokyo
2-30-19 Toshima Ku Ikebukuro Ni Chome +81 3 -5951 -0995

THAILAND

LODGING:

Gay Hotel Paradise Pattaya
Pattaya
https://gay-hotel-pattaya.com/

Gay Nude Sail
https://gaysail.com/

OUTDOORS:

Ao Sane Beach
Nai Harn, Phuket
https://www.phuket101.net/ao-sane-beach/

Freedom Beach
Patong Beach, Phuket
https://www.phuket101.net/freedom-beach/

Karon Beach
Ban Karon, Phuket
https://www.phuket101.net/karon-beach/

Kata Beach
Ban Karon, Phuket
https://www.phuket101.net/kata-beach/

Patong Beach
Patong Beach, Phuket
https://www.phuket101.net/patong-beach/

Ya Nui Beach

Nai Harn, Phuket
https://www.phuket101.net/ya-nui-beach/

AUSTRALIA &
NEW ZEALAND

AUSTRALIA

New South Wales

OUTDOORS:

Sydney

Belongil Beach
Sydney
Byron Bay
https://byronbay.com/belongil-beach-byron-bay/

Cobbler's Nude Beach
Sydney,
https://www.nationalparks.nsw.gov.au/things-to-do/
swimming-spots/cobblers-beach

King's Beach
Sydney, Byron Bay
https://www.byron-bay-beaches.com/kings-beach.html

Lady Bay Beach
Sydney
https://www.nationalparks.nsw.gov.au/things-to-do/
swimming-spots/lady-bay-beach

Obelisk Beach
Sydney
Sydney Harbour National Park (behind Middle Head)
https://www.worldbeachguide.com/australia/obelisk-beach.htm

Washaway Beach

Sydney
https://www.worldbeachguide.com/australia/washaway-
beach.htm

Other cities

Birdie Beach
Budgewoi
Munmorah State Conservation
https://www.worldbeachguide.com/australia/birdie-beach.htm

Flint and Steel Beach
Forestville
Ku-ring-gai Chase National Park, Ettalong Beach
https://www.nationalparks.nsw.gov.au/things-to-do/walking-
tracks/flint-and-steel-track

Jibbon Beach
Little Jibbon
Royal National Park
https://www.worldbeachguide.com/australia/jibbon-beach.htm

Marley Beach
Bundeena
https://www.nationalparks.nsw.gov.au/things-to-do/walking-
tracks/bundeena-drive-to-marley-walk

Miners Beach
Port Macquarie
https://www.nps.gov/places/miners-beach.htm

One Mile Beach @ Samurai Beach
Newcastle
Tomaree National Park
https://www.nationalparks.nsw.gov.au/things-to-do/surfing-
spots/samurai-beach

Seven Mile Beach
Berry

Seven Mile Beach National Park
https://berry.org.au/explore/seven-mile-beach/

Werrong Beach
Otford
Royal National Park
https://www.nationalparks.nsw.gov.au/things-to-do/walking-tracks/werrong-beach-track

WELLNESS:

Men's Naked Yoga, Massage, and Sexological Bodywork & Workshops
Sydney
https://bodycurious.com

Dabaco Sunset
Sydney
http://dabacosunset.com/

Nakedman
Sydney
https://nman.com.au

Naked Yoga Sydney - St. Peters
Sydney, New South Wales
https://www.nakedyogasydney.com

Woof Club
Sydney
https://www.woofclub.com/

Queensland

LODGING:

Hideaway Noosa Men's Beach Resort
Peregian Beach, Queensland
http://www.hideawaymensresort.net/index.html

Turtle Cove Beach Resort

Port Douglas/Wangetti, Queensland
https://turtlecove.com
(LGBTQIA+, check calendar for men-only events)

OUTDOORS:

Alexandria Bay (A-bay) - Noosa Beach
Noosa
National Park, Queensland
https://www.noosa.com/alexandria-bay/

Cow Bay Beach
Port Douglas, Queensland
Draintree Rainforest
https://www.worldbeachguide.com/australia/cow-bay.htm

South Australia

OUTDOORS:

Maslin Beach
Adelaide
(The 1.5km southern end of the beach permits full nudity.)
https://www.worldbeachguide.com/australia/maslin-beach.htm

Tasmania

OUTDOORS:

Baker's Beach
Port Sorell
https://www.worldbeachguide.com/australia/bakers-beach.htm

Victoria

OUTDOORS:

Point Impossible
Torquay
261 Esplanade
https://beachsafe.org.au/beach/vic/greater-geelong/breamlea/

point-impossible

Point Addis
Bells Beach
Ironbark Track
https://www.parks.vic.gov.au/places-to-see/parks/point-addis-marine-national-park

Sunnyside North Beach
Melbourne
Mornington Peninsula
https://www.worldbeachguide.com/australia/sunnyside-beach.htm

WELLNESS:

Gay Men's Yoga
Melbourne, Collingwood
https://www.gaymensyoga.com.au

Nakedman
Melbourne
https://nman.com.au

Woof Club
Melbourne
https://www.woofclub.com/

Western Australia

OUTDOORS:

North Swanbourne Beach
Perth
https://www.worldbeachguide.com/australia/swanbourne-beach.htm

Warnbro Beach
Warnbro
https://www.worldbeachguide.com/australia/warnbro-

beach.htm

Mauritius Beach

Dampier, Exmouth Peninsula
https://www.worldbeachguide.com/australia/mauritius-beach.htm

Cable Beach

Broome
https://www.australiasnorthwest.com/explore/broome-dampier-peninsula/broome/broome-beaches/cable-beach

WELLNESS:

Eric Scwartz Yoga

Subiaco, Western Australia
https://www.nakedyogaaustralia.com.au

Woof Club

Perth
https://www.woofclub.com/

NEW ZEALAND

LODGING:

Guysers Rotorua
Rotorua, North Island
https://guysers.co.nz

Autumn Farm
Golden Bay, South Island
http://www.autumnfarm.com/index.html
(LGBTQIA+)

OUTDOORS:

Breaker Beach
Wellington City, Wellington
https://sandee.com/new-zealand/wellington/wellington/
breaker-bay

Karekare Beach
Waitakere, Auckland
https://www.worldbeachguide.com/new-zealand/karekare-
beach.htm

Ladies Bay Beach
St Helier's, Auckland
https://sandee.com/new-zealand/auckland/st-heliers/ladies-bay-
beach

Little Palm Beach
Waiheke Island, Auckland
https://www.worldbeachguide.com/new-zealand/little-palm-

beach.htm

Papamoa Beach
Tauranga, Bay of Plenty
https://www.holidayparks.co.nz/park/tasman-holiday-parks-papamoa-beach/

Peka Peka Beach
Waikanae, Wellington
https://www.worldbeachguide.com/new-zealand/peka-peka-beach.htm

Pohutukawa Beach
Okura, Auckland
https://beachnearby.com/en-US/beach/pohutukawa-bay-hibiscus-coast-auckland

St Leonard's Bay
North Shore, Auckland
https://www.worldbeachguide.com/new-zealand/saint-leonards-beach.htm

Uretiti Beach
Waipu, Northland
https://www.freebeaches.org.nz/uretiti.htm

Waikuku Beach
Christchurch, Canterbury (South Island)
https://www.christchurchnz.info/business/waikuku-beach

CARIBBEAN

ANTIGUA

OUTDOORS:

Hawksbill Bay
St. John's / Hawksbill Bay
https://hawksbillresortantigua.com/?
gclid=CjwKCAjwhJukBhBPEiwAniIcNXBa_NX_hMy6dU1I8ZG6qX
Zbn0HbhzpCSjOjl-_m9xabdMpUZQKyNRoCBlQQAvD_BwE

CUBA

OUTDOORS:

Mi Cayito
Playa de Esta, Havana
https://www.rainbowgetaways.net/post/best-gay-beaches-in-the-caribbean

GUADALOUPE

OUTDOORS:

Plage Anse Tarare
Saint François
https://www.gay-sejour.com/en/a-8800/anse-tarare.html

Plage Gay Naturiste de Sainte Rose
Canton de Sainte-Rose
https://www.gay-sejour.com/fr/a-8804/plage-gay-naturiste-de-sainte-rose.html

MARTINIQUE

OUTDOORS:

Plage de la Petite Anse des Saline
Sainte-Anne
https://www.worldbeachguide.com/caribbean/petite-anse-salines.htm

PUERTO RICO

OUTDOORS:

Boquillas Beach
Natural Reserve, Hacienda La Esperanza, Manati
https://roampuertorico.com/things-to-do/boquillas-beach-
puerto-rico/#:~:text=Nude%20beaches%20in%20Puerto
%20Rico,the%20small%20municipality%20of%20Manat
%C3%AD

SAINT BARTHS

OUTDOORS:

Anse de Grand Saline
Gustavia
https://www.worldbeachguide.com/caribbean/grande-saline-beach.htm

Gouvetneur Beach
Gustavia
https://www.worldbeachguide.com/caribbean/gouverneur-beach.htm

SINT MAARTEN

OUTDOORS:

Cupecoy Beach
Cupecoy Bay (French / Dutch border)
https://www.sint-maarten.net/place/beach/cupecoy

Happy Bay Beach
Friar's Bay
https://www.sint-maarten.net/place/beach/happy-bay

Orient Beach
Marigot
https://www.worldbeachguide.com/caribbean/orient-beach.htm

EUROPE

AUSTRIA

WELLNESS:

Eros Touch Ritual
Vienna
https://www.erostouchritual.com/

BELGIUM

OUTDOORS:

Plage de Bredene
Bredene
https://bredene.be/fr/plage-naturiste

CROATIA

LODGING:

Gay Nude Sail
https://gaysail.com/

Salty Boys
https://saltyboys.com/

OUTDOORS:

Duilovo Beach
Split
https://www.worldbeachguide.com/croatia/plaza-za-pse-duilovo.htm

Kasjun Beach
Split
https://beachsearcher.com/en/beach/191201548/kasjuni-beach

Jarun Lake
Zagreb
https://www.viator.com/Zagreb-attractions/Jarun-Lake/overview/d5391-a12319

FKK Rocks Lokrum Island
Dubrovnik
https://www.cronatur.com/beach/bdlokrum.htm

Jerolim Island
Hvar
https://www.hvarboats.com/en/places/jerolim

Punta Križa Gay Beach
Rovinj
http://www.rovinj.co/meet-rovinj/beaches/swinger-gay/

DENMARK

OUTDOORS:

Albuen Strand
Nakskov
https://www.worldbeachguide.com/denmark/albuen-
strand.htm

Bellevue Beach/ Klampenborg
Klampenborg - outskirts of Denmark
https://www.visitcopenhagen.com/copenhagen/planning/
bellevue-gdk482349

Bøtøskoven
Lolland-Falster
https://www.visitlolland-falster.com/tourist/highlights/beaches

Brøndby Strand
Sjælland
https://strandguide.dk/broendby-strand/

Strandlund Nudist Beach
Charlottenlund Fort/
https://strandguide.dk/charlottenlund-fortstrandlund/

Grenå (Annabjerg Plantation)
East Jutland
https://strandguide.dk/grenaa-annebjerg-plantage/

Den Permanente Århus
Rissov
https://www.worldbeachguide.com/denmark/den-

permanente.htm

Erikshale Nudist Beach
Marstal
https://www.worldbeachguide.com/denmark/eriks-hale.htm

Embarrassed Beach
Southern Jutland
https://strandguide.dk/flovt-strand/

Hvide Sande Beach
Hvide Sande
https://www.visitvesterhavet.com/northsea/north-sea-
vacation/hvide-sande-sydstrand-gdk602903

Houstrup Strand
North Jutland
https://strandguide.dk/kaersgaard-strand/

Kærsdaard Strand
NorthJutland
https://strandguide.dk/kaersgaard-strand/

Klitmøller Strand
Klitøller
https://www.visitnordvestkysten.dk/nordvestkysten/planlaeg-
din-tur/klitmoeller-strand-gdk601444

Måle Strand (Measuring Beach)
Funen
https://strandguide.dk/maale-strand/

Rødhus Kærsgaard Beach
North Jutland
https://www.worldbeachguide.com/denmark/rodhus-
strand.htm

Rømø Bilstrand
Rømø
https://www.beachrex.com/en/denmark/syddanmark/romo-

beaches/strand-lakolk

Skagen-Damsterderne
Northe Jutland
https://strandguide.dk/skagen-damstederne/

Skomose Strand
Jylland
https://www.visitsonderjylland.dk/turist/information/
skovmose-strand-gdk611507

Thurø Reef
Fyn
https://www.visitfyn.com/fyn/cities-and-islands/thuro

Tisvilde Beach
Tisvilde
https://www.visitnorthsealand.com/north-sealand/events/
tisvildeleje-beach-gdk964060

Vesterlyng
Sjælland
https://www.visitdenmark.com/denmark/explore/eskebjerg-
vesterlyng-beach-gdk638390

FINLAND

OUTDOORS:

Yyteri Naturist Beach (Yyterin Hiekkarantaa)
Pori - Golf of Bothnia
https://www.worldbeachguide.com/finland/yyterin-naturistiranta.htm

FRANCE

LODGING:
Les Vieles Tentes
Saint-Romain-de-Lerps, Auvergne-Rhône-Alpes
https://les-vieilles-tentes-49.webself.net/?utm_source=gay-sejour&utm_medium=referral

Le Vieux Donjon
Pressigny-les-Pins, Centre-Val de Loire
https://www.gayresort-hotel.com/

South of France

Aloha
Bessan, Occitaina
http://www.chambres-gay-herault-aloha.fr/en/index.html

Cinq & Sept
Roujan, Occitania
https://www.cinqetsept.com

La Mariette
Ambax, Occitainia
https://www.lamariette.fr/en/

Villa Litoral
Le Grau d'Agde, Occitania
http://www.villalittoral.com/site/eg_accueil.html

The Lotus Tree
Montclus, Occitania
http://thelotustree.com

Villa Casada
Agde, Occitainia
http://www.villacascada.fr/

Villa Ragazzi
Uchaud, Occitaina
https://en.villaragazzi.com

Le Connexion
Peymeinade/ Ca, Provence-Alpes-Côte d'Azur
https://laconnexion.eu/en/

Villa Bacchus
Vidauban, Provence-Alpes-Côte d'Azur
http://villa-bacchus.voyage/en/

Salty Boys - cruise
https://saltyboys.com/

OUTDOORS:

Brittany

Beach Porzh Aour
Crozon
https://www.beachatlas.com/porzh-aour

Kerminihy Beach
Étal
https://www.worldbeachguide.com/france/kerminihy.htm

Le Lortuais Gay Beach
Le Portuais / Erquy
https://www.google.com/search?client=safari&rls=en&q=Le
+Lortuais+Gay+Beach&ie=UTF-8&oe=UTF-8

Plage du Verger
Saint-Malo
https://www.beachatlas.com/verger

Naturist Beach Les Jaunts
Saint-Nazaine
https://en.plages.tv/detail/jaunais-beach-saint-nazaire-44600

Corsica

Aregno
Algajona
https://www.beachatlas.com/aregno

Bagheera Naturist Beach
Linguizzetta
https://www.beachatlas.com/bagheera-beach

Bella Riva Beach (Riva Bella spa center)
Linguizzetta
https://www.beachatlas.com/bella-riva-beach

Bodri Beach
L'île-Rousse
https://www.beachatlas.com/bodri-beach

Cala d'Aguila
Belevedere Campomoro
https://www.beachatlas.com/cala-aguila

Capitello Beach
Porticcio
https://en.plages.tv/detail/capitello-beach-porticcio-20128

Canusellu Beach
Belevedere Campomoro
https://www.beachatlas.com/canusellu-beach

Chiappa Beach
Porto Vecchio
https://www.beachatlas.com/chiappa-beach

Chiosura Beach
Linguizzetta

https://www.beachatlas.com/chiosura-beach

Grand Capo Beach
Ajaccio
https://www.beachatlas.com/grand-capo-beach

Linguizzetta Beach
Corsica
The east coast of Corsica, nude all the way from the naturist resort just north of the Étang de Diane lagoon until you reach the little town of Bravone.
https://en.plages.tv/detail/beach-linguizzetta-20232

Ricanto Beach (Tahiti Beach)
Ajaccio
https://www.beachatlas.com/ricanto-and-tahiti-beach

San Giuseppe Beach
Sagone
https://www.beachatlas.com/san-giuseppe-beach

Stagnolu Beach
Bonifacio
https://www.beachatlas.com/stagnolu-beach

Tropica Beach
Linguizzetta
https://www.beachatlas.com/tropica-beach

Gaillan-en-Médoc

Montalivet Naturist Beach (Monta Beach)
Gaillan-en-Médoc
https://www.worldbeachguide.com/france/montalivet-naturist-beach.htm

Hauts-de-France

Berch-sur-Mer des Sables d'Opale
Picardy

https://francetravelblog.com/best-nudist-beaches-in-france/

Terminus Beach
Berck
Esp. Parmentier, 62600
https://www.beachrex.com/en/france/hauts-de-france/berck-beaches/plage-de-terminus?bt=family-beaches

Normandy

Biville Gay Beach
Biville-Sur-Mer/Petit-Caux
https://nudistcompass.com/place/83

La Redoute Beach
Merville-Franceville-Plage
Normandy
https://nudistcompass.com/place/81

Noulvelle-Aquitaine

Arnaoutchot Naturist Beach
Vielle-Saint-Girons
https://www.nakedwanderings.com/review-arnaoutchot-in-vieille-saint-girons-france/

Hossegor
Aquitaine
https://en.plages.tv/detail/naturist-beach-hossegor-40150

La Jenny Beach
La Porge
https://www.worldbeachguide.com/france/la-jenny.htm

La Palmyre Beach
La Palmyre
https://www.guide-charente-maritime.com/en/tourism/discover/the-beaches-of-charente-maritime/les-mathes-447/-

palmyre-beach-10084.html

Plage Naturiste de Montalivet
Vendays-Montalivet
https://www.plages.tv/detail/plage-sud-vendays-montalivet-33930

Loire-Atlantique

Plage de Kerger
Fouesnant
https://www.worldbeachguide.com/france/plage-de-kerler.htm

South of France

Occitania

Cap d'Agde Naturist Beach
Le Cap d'Agde
https://www.worldbeachguide.com/france/cap-d-agde.htm
One part of a larger naturist resort in the south-coast town of Agde, near Montpellier

Eastern Beach
Saintes-Maries-de-la-Mer
https://www.beachatlas.com/eastern-beach

Espiguette
Le Grau-du-Rio / Port Camargue
https://www.beachatlas.com/espiguette

La Grande Cosse
Lanuedoc
Between Grande Cosse and neighbouring Pissevaches Beach.
https://www.naturist-holiday-guide.com/la-grande-cosse.html

Mont Rose Beach
Marseille
Avenue de la Montedon
https://www.travelgay.com/venue/mont-rose-beach/

Plage Naturiste Port Leucate
Leucate
https://www.worldbeachguide.com/france/port-leucate-naturist-beach.htm

Serignan Plage
Serignan
https://en.plages.tv/detail/naturist-beach-serignan-34410

Provence-Alpes-Côte d'Azur

Bau Rouges Beach
Carqueiranne
https://www.beachatlas.com/bau-rouges-beach

Beach de la Batterie Basse
Toulon
https://www.beachatlas.com/batterie-basse

Beach de la Mitre
Toulon
https://www.beachatlas.com/mitre

Beach des Brouis
La Croix-Valmer
https://www.beachatlas.com/brouis

Beach des Esclamandes
Fréjus
https://www.beachatlas.com/esclamandes

Boeuf Beach
La Seyne-sur-Mer
https://www.beachatlas.com/boeuf-beach

Bonnieu's Naturist Beach
Martigues
https://www.beachatlas.com/bonnieus-naturist-beach

Calanque of Athénors

Ensuès-la-Redonne
https://www.beachatlas.com/calanque-of-athenors

Cap Roux Naturist Beach
Cannes
https://www.beachatlas.com/cap-roux-naturist-beach

Castel Plage
Nice
Quai des États-Unis, 06300
https://en.plageprivee.com/france/06-alpes-maritimes/nice/
castel-plage

Criques du Cap Estel
Èze
https://www.beachatlas.com/criques-du-cap-estel

Dugue Beach
Ensuès-la-Redonne
https://www.beachatlas.com/dugue-beach

Gigaro Beach
Saint Tropez
https://www.beachatlas.com/gigaro-beach

Naturist Coves*
Cavalaire-sur-Mer
RN559, in front of the campsite "Bon Porteau"
https://www.cavalairesurmer.fr/cote-mer/cote-plages/la-plage-
de-bonporteau.html

Douane Creek
Saint-Topez
https://www.beachatlas.com/douane-creek

Jean Blanc Beach
Le Lavandou
https://www.beachatlas.com/jean-blanc-beach

Jovat Beach

La Croix-Valmer
https://www.beachatlas.com/jovat-beach

Layet Beach
Le Lavandou
https://www.beachatlas.com/layet-beach

Layet Creek
Le Lavandou
https://www.beachatlas.com/nudist-beaches-france

Les Gottes - île du Levant (Plage des Gottes)
Le Lavandou
https://www.worldbeachguide.com/france/plage-des-grottes.htm

Lighthouse Beach
Saint-Jean-Cap-Ferrat / Nice
https://www.beachatlas.com/lighthouse-beach

Liouquet Beach
La Ciotat
https://www.beachatlas.com/liouquet-beach

Pampelonne Beach
Saint-Tropez
https://www.beachatlas.com/pampelonne-beach

Pissarelles Beach
Èze
https://www.beachatlas.com/pissarelles-beach

Plage de Piémanson (Plage d'Arles)
Salin-de-Giraud, Port-Saint-Louis-du-Rhône
https://www.beachatlas.com/piemanson

Plage de la Moutte
Saint-Tropez
https://www.beachatlas.com/moutte

Plateforme Beach
Nice
https://www.beachatlas.com/plateforme-beach

Rochers du Dramont
La Dramont - Saint Raphael / Cannes
https://en.plages.tv/detail/rochers-du-dramont-cathedral-beach-saint-raphael-83700

Salins Beach - Pentagon Beach
Hyères
https://www.beachatlas.com/salins-beach-pentagon-beach

Saint-Selon Naturist Beach
Toulon
On the edge of Janas Forest, close to La Seyne-sur-Mer.
https://www.worldbeachguide.com/france/plage-naturiste-de-saint-selon.htm

Tahiti Nudist Beach
Saint-Tropez
It's part of the larger Pampelonne Beach.
https://www.worldbeachguide.com/france/plage-de-tahiti.htm

WELLNESS:

Nude Yoga Paris
https://www.yoga-arcenciel.com

L'impact Nude Bar
Paris
18 Rue Greneta

GERMANY

LODGING:

Deutsche Eiche Munich
Munich
https://www.deutsche-eiche.de/en/

OUTDOORS:

Absberg Naturist Beach (FKK Strand Absberg)
Absberg, Bavaria
Seespitz, 91720 Absberg
http://www.nakedplaces.net/photos/
de_by_mf_kleiner_brombachsee.html

Buhne 16 and Kampen, Sylt
Adjoining beaches of Buhne 16 and Kampen
Listlandstrasse, 25999 Kampen (Sylt)
https://www.beach-inspector.com/en/b/buhne-16

Duhnen Beach (Strand Duhnen)
Duhnen, Cuxhaven
Dünenweg 12, 27476 Cuxhaven
https://beachsearcher.com/en/beach/276201010/duhnen-
strand

Flaucher FKK Strand (on the Isar riverside in Munich)
Flaucher, Munich
Flauchersteg, Flauchersteg, 81379 Munich
https://nudistcompass.com/place/997

Lake of Wannsee

Wannsee, 14109 Berlin
https://faraway.life/2017/08/15/wannsee-strandbad-the-lake-where-berliners-go-when-they-miss-the-sea/

The Naturist Lido of Müggelsee (FKK Strandbad Müggelsee)
Müggelsee, Berlin
Strandbad Müggelsee, Fürstenwalder Damm 838, 12589 Berlin
https://activenaturists.net/2014/09/19/muggelsee/

Ording Nord Naturist Beach (Badestelle Ording Nord FKK)
Ording Nord, Schleswig-Holstein
25826 Sankt Peter-Ording
https://www.beach-inspector.com/en/b/badestelle-ording-nord-fkk

Pohl Dam Naturist Beach (Talsperre Pöhl FKK Strand)
Talsperre Pöhl, Saxony
Pöhler Str. 19, 08543 Pöhl
https://zekaa.com/pohl-dam-nudist-beach

Priwall Naturist Beach (FKK Strand Priwall)
Priwall, Lübeck
Seeweg 131, 23570 Lübeck
https://www.beach-inspector.com/en/b/strand-priwall

Strand am Unterbacher See
Nudist beach at the Lake in Unterbach
https://naked-adventure.eu/place/strandbad-sud-unterbacher-see

Mecklenburg-Vorpommern

Ahlbeck Naturist Beach (FKK Strand Ahlbeck)
Ahlbeck, Usedom
Ahlbeck Beach, Heringsdorf, Germany
https://www.beachatlas.com/ahlbeck

Ahrenshoop Beach
Ahrenshoop

https://www.beachatlas.com/nudist-beaches-mecklenburg-vorpommern

Binz Beach
Binz, Rugen
https://www.beachatlas.com/binz-beach

Breege Ost
Breege
https://www.beachatlas.com/breege-ost

Dierhagen Beach
Dierhagen
https://www.beachatlas.com/dierhagen-beach

Heiligendamm Beach
Bad Doberan, Rostock
https://www.beachatlas.com/heiligendamm

Hohe Düne
Rostock
https://www.beachatlas.com/hohe-dune

Kühlungsborn Beach
Kühlungsborn
https://www.beachatlas.com/kuhlungsborn-beach

Mukran Beach
Binz, Rügen
https://www.beachatlas.com/mukran

Prora Beach
Binz, Rügen
https://www.beachatlas.com/prora

Sellin Beach
Island of Rügen
https://www.beachatlas.com/selling-beach

Warnemünde Naturist Beach (FKK Strand Warnemünde)

Rostock / Warnemünde, Mecklenburg-Vorpommern
Seestraße, 18119 Rostock
https://www.beach-inspector.com/en/b/badestelle-ording-nord-fkk

Zierow
Zierow
https://www.beachatlas.com/zierow-beach

Zinnowitz Beach
Zinnowitz, Usedom
https://www.beachatlas.com/zinnowitz-beach

WELLNESS:

Eros Touch Ritual
Berlin
https://www.erostouchritual.com/

GREECE

LODGING:

Gay Nude Sail
https://gaysail.com/

Salty Boys
https://saltyboys.com/

OUTDOORS:

Crete

Agios Pavlos
Crete
https://beachsearcher.com/en/beach/300227323/agios-pavlos-beach

Agia Roumeli
Crete
http://www.greek-islands.us/crete/crete-nudist /

Ammoudi
Crete
http://www.greek-islands.us/crete/crete-nudist/

Elafonissi Beach
Chania, Crete
https://www.beachatlas.com/elafonissi-beach

Filaki Beach
Crete
http://www.greek-islands.us/crete/crete-nudist/

Gavdos Beach
Crete
http://www.greek-islands.us/crete/crete-nudist /

Glyka Nera
Crete
http://www.greek-islands.us/crete/crete-nudist/

Komos Beach
Crete
https://www.matala-holidays.com/en/komos-beach

Livadi Beach
Bali, Crete
https://www.beachatlas.com/livadi-beach

Lentas Beach
Crete
http://www.greek-islands.us/crete/crete-nudist/

Maltata Beach
Maltata, Crete
https://www.beachatlas.com/matala-beach

Palaiochora Beach
Crete
http://www.greek-islands.us/crete/crete-nudist/

Plakias Beach
Crete
http://www.greek-islands.us/crete/crete-nudist/

Stalis Beach
Malia
https://www.beachatlas.com/stalis-beach

Red Beach
Matala, Crete
https://www.worldbeachguide.com/greece/red-beach.htm

Sougia Beach
Crete
http://www.greek-islands.us/crete/crete-nudist

Corfu

Acharavi Beach
Corfu
https://acharavi-corfu.com/

Agios Stefanos Beach
Corfu
https://seaspiration.com/greece-beach-vacation-tips/corfu-nudist-beaches/

Almyros Beach
Corfu
https://seaspiration.com/greece-beach-vacation-tips/corfu-nudist-beaches/

Arillas Beach
Corfu
https://seaspiration.com/greece-beach-vacation-tips/corfu-nudist-beaches/

Arkoudilas Beach
Cavos, Corfu
https://www.beachatlas.com/arkoudilas-beach

Glyfada Beach
Corfu
https://seaspiration.com/greece-beach-vacation-tips/corfu-nudist-beaches/

Halikounas Beach
Corfu
https://seaspiration.com/greece-beach-vacation-tips/corfu-nudist-beaches/

Paradise Beach
Palaiokastritsa, Corfu
https://www.beachatlas.com/paradise-beach3

Myrtiotissa Beach
Corfu
https://www.worldbeachguide.com/greece/myrtiotissa-beach.htm

Mykonos

Agios Sostis
Mykonos
https://www.beachatlas.com/agios-sostis-beach

Elia Beach
Mykonos
https://www.mykonosbeachesguide.com/beaches/elia-beach.html

Fokos
Mykonos
https://www.beachatlas.com/fokos-beach

Korfos
Mykonos
https://www.beachatlas.com/korfos-beach

Megali Ammos
Mykonos
https://www.beachatlas.com/megali-ammos-beach

Merchais
Mykonos
https://www.beachatlas.com/merchias

Paradise Beach
Mykonos
https://mykonostraveller.com/listings/paradise-beach-

mykonos/

Psarou
Mykonos
https://www.beachatlas.com/psarou-beach

Saint Anna
Mykonos
https://www.beachatlas.com/saint-anna-beach

Super Paradise
Mykonos
https://www.mykonosbeachesguide.com/beaches/super-paradise-beach.html

Kos

Polemi Beach
Kos City
https://www.beachatlas.com/polemi

Psalidi
Kos City
https://www.beachatlas.com/psalidi-beach

Naxos

Agia Marina Beach
Naxos
https://www.greeka.com/cyclades/milos/beaches/agia-marina/

Plaka Beach
Naxos
https://www.greeka.com/cyclades/naxos/beaches/plaka/

Plakias

Plakias Beach
Plakias
https://www.beachatlas.com/plakias-beach

Prevail Beach
Plakias
https://www.beachatlas.com/preveli-beach

Rhodes

Faliraki Beach
Rhodes
https://www.greeka.com/dodecanese/rhodes/beaches/faliraki-nudist/

Tsambika Beach
Kolymbia
https://www.beachatlas.com/tsambika-beach

Other

Ai Gianna
Gavdos
https://greeking.me/blog/tips/nudist-beaches-in-greece

Little Banana
Skiathos
https://www.whichgreekisland.co.uk/islands/skiathos/beaches/little-banana/

Camping Beach
Antiparos
https://www.feelgreece.com/en/camping-beach-antiparos

Chilladou Nude Beach
Evoia
https://www.greece.com/photos/destinations/Central_Greece/Evia/Settlement/Chiliadou_Beach/Hiliadou_nudist_beach,_Evia_island,_Greece/24582210

Gypsoi Afiarti Beach
Karpathos
https://greeking.me/blog/tips/nudist-beaches-in-greece

Kedros Beach
Donousa
https://www.greeka.com/cyclades/donoussa/beaches/kendros/

Tsamadou Beach
Samos
https://www.worldbeachguide.com/greece/tsamadou.htm

Velanio
Skopelos
http://www.skopelostravel.net/beaches/velanio/

WELLNESS:

Eros Touch Ritual
Mykonos
https://www.erostouchritual.com/

IRELAND

OUTDOORS:

<u>**Co. Clare**</u>

Kilkee Beach (north end)
Kilkee
https://irishnaturistblog.wordpress.com/index-of-irish-
naturist-beaches/

Lough Greany Lake
Flagmount
https://irishnaturistblog.wordpress.com/index-of-irish-
naturist-beaches/

<u>**Co. Cork**</u>

Clonakitty Bay
Dunny, Sands, Prison, Simon's Coves
https://irishnaturistblog.wordpress.com/index-of-irish-
naturist-beaches/

Long Strand
Owenachna
https://irishnaturistblog.wordpress.com/index-of-irish-
naturist-beaches/

<u>**Co. Dublin**</u>

Corballis
Donabate
https://irishnaturistblog.wordpress.com/index-of-irish-

naturist-beaches/

The Forty Foot
Dun Laoghoire
https://irishnaturistblog.wordpress.com/index-of-irish-
naturist-beaches/

Vico Road
Dalkey
https://irishnaturistblog.wordpress.com/index-of-irish-
naturist-beaches/

<u>Co. Galway</u>

Dog's Bay
Roundstone
https://www.irelandbeforeyoudie.com/the-5-best-known-
nudist-beaches-in-ireland-ranked/

Silver Strand Beach
Galway / Barca
https://www.thebeachguide.co.uk/republic-of-ireland/county-
galway/silverstrand.htm

<u>Co. Kerry</u>

Banna Strand
Ballyheige Bay
https://irishnaturistblog.wordpress.com/index-of-irish-
naturist-beaches/

Beal Strand
Beal Point / Ballybunion
https://irishnaturistblog.wordpress.com/index-of-irish-
naturist-beaches/

Clogher Beach
Dingle Peninsula
https://irishnaturistblog.wordpress.com/index-of-irish-

naturist-beaches/

Inch
Dingle Peninsula
https://irishnaturistblog.wordpress.com/index-of-irish-naturist-beaches/

Murreagh Strand
Dingle Peninsula
https://irishnaturistblog.wordpress.com/index-of-irish-naturist-beaches/

Stradbally Strand
Dingle Peninsula
https://irishnaturistblog.wordpress.com/index-of-irish-naturist-beaches/

Ventry Beach (third enterance)
Ventry
https://irishnaturistblog.wordpress.com/index-of-irish-naturist-beaches/

Co. Mayo

Bartraw
Westport Bay
https://irishnaturistblog.wordpress.com/index-of-irish-naturist-beaches/

Keem Strand
Achill Island
https://irishnaturistblog.wordpress.com/index-of-irish-naturist-beaches/

Old Head
Clew Bay
https://irishnaturistblog.wordpress.com/index-of-irish-naturist-beaches/

Trawmore Sand

Achill Island
https://irishnaturistblog.wordpress.com/index-of-irish-naturist-beaches/

Co Sligo

Trawalua Strand
West Mullaghmore Head
https://irishnaturistblog.wordpress.com/index-of-irish-naturist-beaches/

Yellow Strand
Sligo Bay / Drumcliff Bay
https://irishnaturistblog.wordpress.com/index-of-irish-naturist-beaches/

Co. Waterford

Caliso Bay
Monatray
https://www.thebeachguide.co.uk/republic-of-ireland/county-waterford/caliso-bay.htm

Co. Wexford

Curracloe
South Curracloe Beach
https://irishnaturistblog.wordpress.com/index-of-irish-naturist-beaches/

Co. Wicklow

Brittas Bay
Magheramore north of Britts Bay.
Sallymount south of Brittas Bay.
https://irishnaturistblog.wordpress.com/index-of-irish-naturist-beaches/

ITALY

LODGING:

Bellaugello
Gubbio PG, Itally
https://bellaugello.com

Salty Boys
https://saltyboys.com/

OUTDOORS:

Abruzzo

Spiaggia Naturista Lido Punta Le Morge
SS 16 Adriatica, 66020 Torino di Sangro, Chieti
https://naturistitalia.it/punta-le-morge/

Apulia

Spiaggia della Commenda
Commenda di Maruggio
near Taranto in Puglia
 https://www.italianaturista.it/altre-spiagge-naturiste/spiaggia-della-commenda-ta

Emilia - Romagna

Spiaggia della Bassona
Viale Paolo e Francesca, 48124 Ravenna, Lido di Dante
https://www.italianaturista.it/spiagge-autorizzate/lido-di-dante-spiaggia-della-bassona-ra

Lazio

Oasi Naturista di Capocotta Beach - Il Buco Beach
Via del Lido di Castel Porziano
(between Settimo Cielo and Meterranea restaurants)
Pomezia - Capocotta Nature Reserve
 https://www.worldbeachguide.com/italy/oasi-naturista-di-capocotta.htm

Liguria

Chiavari Beach
Genoa
https://www.beachatlas.com/chiavari

Guvano Beach
Vernazza, La Spezia
https://www.worldbeachguide.com/italy/guvano.htm

Marche

Spiaggia Sassi Neri (San Michelle)
Piazza Vittorio Veneto, 20, 60020 Sirolo / Ancona
https://beachsearcher.com/en/beach/380401035/spiaggia-sassi-neri

Salerno

Spiaggia del Troncone FKK
Via Mingardo, 84059 Marina di Camerota, Salerno
https://www.italianaturista.it/spiagge-autorizzate/spiaggia-del-troncone-marina-di-camerota-sa

Sardina

Is Benas
Aritanis Oristano
https://beachsearcher.com/en/beach/380221270/spiaggia-di-is-benas

Porto Ferro Beach
Olmeda
https://www.worldbeachguide.com/italy/porto-ferro.htm

Spiaggia di Piscinas
09031 Arbus, South Sardinia, Italy
https://www.worldbeachguide.com/italy/piscinas.htm

Sicily

Riserva Naturale di Capo Gallo
Palermo
https://www.worldbeachguide.com/italy/capo-gallo-beach.htm

Spiaggia di Marianelli
Noto
https://www.worldbeachguide.com/italy/spiaggia-di-marianelli.htm

Torre Salsa Mature Preserve
Montenegro
https://www.worldbeachguide.com/italy/torre-salsa.htm

Trieste

Spiaggia Costa dei Barbari FKK
Località Sistiana, 34011 Sistiana / Trieste
https://www.italianaturista.it/altre-spiagge-naturiste/costa-dei-barbari-sistiana-ts

Tuscany

La Feniglia Beach
Orbetello
https://www.worldbeachguide.com/italy/spiaggia-della-feniglia.htm

Lago di Castelruggero
Chianti

https://nudistcompass.com/place/476

Lecciona Beach
Nature Park of Migliarino – Massaciuccoli - San Rossore
Viareggio
https://www.worldbeachguide.com/italy/naturist-beach-lecciona.htm

Spiaggia di Acquarilli
Cappliveri, Elba Island
https://www.worldbeachguide.com/italy/acquarilli-naturist-beach.htm

Spiaggia di Capalbio - Spiaggia naturista di Macchiatonda
Grosseto
https://nudistcompass.com/place/480

Spiaggia di Marina di Alberese
Regional Park of Maremma
https://nudistcompass.com/place/478

Veneto

Spiaggia degli Alberoni
Venezia
https://www.worldbeachguide.com/italy/alberoni-venice.htm

NETHERLANDS

LODGING:

Dunez Men Only Resort
Druen
https://www.dunez.nl/english/

Salty Boys
https://saltyboys.com/

Gay Nude Sail
https://gaysail.com/

OUTDOORS:

Zandvoort Nudist Beach
Amsterdam
between poles 68 and 71
https://www.visitzandvoort.com/zandvoort-nudist-beach

Amsterdamse Bos - Zonneweide
Amsterdam Forest Park
https://naaktstrandje.nl/noordholland/AmsterdamseBos/
AmsterdamseBosEngels.html

Nudist Beach Callantsoog
Callantsoog
between poles 14.25 and 16.80
https://www.naaktstrandje.nl/noordholland/callantsoog/
CallantsoogEngels.html

Naaktstrandje Het Twiske - Baaiegatstrand

Oostzaan
https://www.naaktstrandje.nl/noordholland/Twiske/
TwiskeEngels.html

Nudist Beach Bussloo
Gelderland
https://www.naaktstrandje.nl/gelderland/Bussloo/
BusslooEngels.html

Nude Beach Scheveningen
The Hague
between poles 96.5 and 98
https://scheveningenbeach.com/things-to-do-and-see/beach/
nude-beach

WELLNESS:

PlayFull Living
Amsterdam
https://www.playfull-living.com/

Club Church
Amsterdam
Naked Men on Wednesdays
https://www.clubchurch.nl

Nieuwe Zijds - Gay Sauna Amsterdam
Amsterdam
https://www.saunanieuwezijds.nl

NORWAY

OUTDOORS:

Langøyene
Oslo
https://www.scandinavianaturist.org/en/node/179

Svartkulp
Oslo
https://www.scandinavianaturist.org/en/node/178

Gautviken Naturist Area
https://www.scandinavianaturist.org/en/node/372

Glomstadbukta
Gjøvik
https://www.scandinavianaturist.org/en/node/18

Hjertøya
Molde
https://www.scandinavianaturist.org/en/node/188

Hoøya
Steinkjer
https://www.scandinavianaturist.org/en/node/189

Huk Beach (Hukkoden Strand)
Lysaker
https://www.worldbeachguide.com/norway/huk-oslo.htm

Kalvøya
Sandvika

https://www.scandinavianaturist.org/en/node/180

Kollevågen
Bergen
https://www.scandinavianaturist.org/en/node/186

Mauren
Ålesund
https://www.scandinavianaturist.org/en/node/187

Orrestranden
Jæren
https://www.scandinavianaturist.org/en/node/185

Roppestad
Larvik
https://www.scandinavianaturist.org/en/node/182

Skåtangen / Tjøme
Tønsberg
https://www.scandinavianaturist.org/en/node/184

Stykkjevika
Fyresdal
https://www.scandinavianaturist.org/en/node/183

Søm
Kristiansand
https://www.scandinavianaturist.org/en/node/191

PORTUGAL

LODGING:

Casa Risa
Lisbon
https://www.casarisa.com

Villa 3 Caparica
Lisbon
https://www.villa3caparica.com/welcome

Lua Nua
São Teotónio / Zambujeira do Mar
https://www.luanua.pt

OUTDOORS:

<u>Faro</u>

Meia Praia (Rio de Alvor)
Lagos
https://www.worldbeachguide.com/portugal/meia-praia.htm

Praia das Adegas
Aljezur, Costa Vicentina of the Algarve
https://www.travel-in-portugal.com/beaches/praia-das-adegas.htm

Praia do Canavial
Ponta de Piedade, Lagos
https://www.lagosportugaltourism.com/beaches/praia-do-canavial.html

Praia Grande de Pera
Silves
https://www.visitportugal.com/en/node/141956

Praia João de Arens
Alvor
https://www.worldbeachguide.com/portugal/praia-joao-de-arens.htm

Praia de Odeceixe
Aljezor
https://www.worldbeachguide.com/portugal/praia-de-odeceixe.htm

Praia do Submarino
Alvor / Lagos
https://www.worldbeachguide.com/portugal/praia-do-submarino.htm

Praia de Vale Figueiras
Southwest Alentejo and Vicentine Coast Natural Park
https://www.visitalgarve.pt/pt/2122/praia-de-vale-figueiras.aspx

Lisboa

Naturist Beach 19 (Lisbon's Gay Beach)
Costa da Caparica
https://www.lisbonbeachesguide.com/costa-da-caparica/praia-19-gay-beach.html

Naturist Beach Adiça
Costa da Caparica
https://www.lisbonbeachesguide.com/costa-da-caparica/praia-da-adica.html

Naturist Beach Rio da Prata
Península Ibérica, Costa da Caparica
https://www.lisbonbeachesguide.com/sesimbra/praia-das-

bicas.html

Praia de Adage
Sintra
https://www.lisbonbeachesguide.com/nude-beaches-in-lisbon-portugal.html

Praia da Aguda
Sintra
https://www.lisbonbeachesguide.com/sintra/praia-da-aguda-beach.html

Praia da Bela Vista
Costa de Caparica (just North of Beach 19)
https://www.lisbonbeachesguide.com/nude-beaches-in-lisbon-portugal.html

Praia da Cresmina
Cascais / Lisbon
https://www.lisbonbeachesguide.com/cascais/praia-da-cresmina.html

Praia do Guincho
Cascais / Lisbon
https://lisbonlisboaportugal.com/lisbon-beaches/Praia-Guincho-beach-lisbon.html

Praia da Ursa
Sintra
https://www.lisbonbeachesguide.com/sintra/praia-da-ursa-beach.html

Setúbal

Praia do Meco (Tranqueira)
Em561 Península Ibérica, Costa da Caparica
https://www.lisbonbeachesguide.com/sesimbra/meco.html

Praia Naturista do Salto
R. Antonio do Monte / Porto Covo

https://www.visitportugal.com/en/NR/exeres/87547682-C28B-41FD-8039-1163B26AFDFB

Praia Grande de Pera
Silves
https://www.visitportugal.com/en/node/141956

Praia de Troia-Mar (Soltoia)
Troia Peninsula
https://www.lisbonbeachesguide.com/troia/

Praia do Magoito
Magoitom Sintra
https://www.lisbonbeachesguide.com/sintra/praia-do-magoito-beach.html

Naturist Beach Rio da Prata
Sesimbra, Costa da Caparica
https://www.lisbonbeachesguide.com/sesimbra/praia-das-bicas.html

WELLNESS

Naked Yoga Lisbon
Lisbon
https://www.nkedyoga.com/

SPAIN

LODGING:

Elite Hotel
Sitges
https://www.elitehotelsitges.com

Finca La Maroma
Málaga
https://fincalamaroma.com

Gay Holiday Spain
Barcelona
https://gayholidayspain.wixsite.com/gayholidayspain

Gay Nude Sail
https://gaysail.com/

Hotel Ritual
Málaga
(nude roof top deck)
https://hotelritualtorremolinos.com/en/

La Cigaliere
Olivella/Stiges
https://www.la-cigaliere-sitges.com/index.php

OUTDOORS:

Andalucía

Bolonia Beach
Zahara de los Atunes

https://www.worldbeachguide.com/spain/bolonia.htm

Cantarrijan Beach
Almuñecar
https://www.inspain.org/en/granada/almunecar/beaches/
cantarrijan/

El Muerto Beach
Almuñecar
https://www.inspain.org/en/granada/almunecar/beaches/el-
muerto/

Playas de Vera
Garrucha
https://www.worldbeachguide.com/spain/vera-playa-playa-el-
playazo.htm

Asturias

Aguilera Beach
Gozón
https://www.inspain.org/en/asturias/gozon/beaches/aguilera/

Ballota Beach
Llanes
https://www.inspain.org/en/asturias/llanes/beaches/ballota/

Barayo Beach
Valdés / Navia
https://www.inspain.org/en/asturias/valdes/beaches/barayo-la-
vega/

Beach of Mexota
Tapia de Casariego
https://www.inspain.org/en/asturias/tapia-de-casariego/
beaches/mexota/

Oleiros Beach
Cudillero
https://www.inspain.org/en/asturias/cudillero/beaches/oleiros/

Peñarruubia Beach
Gijón
https://www.travelguidestar.com/nudist-beaches-in-asturias/

Playón de Bayas
Soto del Barco
https://winetourismspain.com/blog/our-favorite-beaches-north-spain/

Requexinos Beach
Castrillón
https://www.inspain.org/en/asturias/castrillon/beaches/requexinos/

San Martin Beach
Llanes
https://www.inspain.org/en/asturias/llanes/beaches/san-martin/

Serlin Beach
Gijón
https://beachsearcher.com/en/beach/724261400/playa-de-serin

Silence Beach
Cudillero
https://www.travelguidestar.com/nudist-beaches-in-asturias/

Torimbia Beach
Llanes
https://www.inspain.org/en/asturias/llanes/beaches/torimbia/

Vega Beach / Gulpiyuri Beach
Berbes / Vega
https://www.absolutviajes.com/en/oviedo/las-mejores-playas-de-asturias-desde-oviedo/

Balearic Islands

Formentera

Calò des Mort Beach
Sant Francesc de Formentera
https://www.worldbeachguide.com/spain/calo-des-mort.htm

Playa de Ses Illetes
Sant Francesc de Formentera
https://www.worldbeachguide.com/spain/playa-de-ses-illetes.htm

Ibiza

Aquas Blancas Beach
Sant Joan de Labritja
https://www.worldbeachguide.com/spain/agua-blanca-beach.htm

Platja des Cavallet
Ibiza
https://www.ibiza-spotlight.com/beach/es_cavallet_i.htm

Mallorca

Cala Mesquida
Capdepera
https://www.worldbeachguide.com/spain/cala-mesquida-0.htm

Es Trenc Beach
South Mallorca
https://www.mallorca-beaches.com/en/es-trenc/

Playa del Ambolo
Valencia - Xàbia, Alicante
https://www.worldbeachguide.com/spain/cala-del-ambolo.htm

Menorca

Cala Excorxada
Ferreries
https://www.worldbeachguide.com/spain/cala-escorxada.htm

Cala Macarelleta
Ferreries
https://www.worldbeachguide.com/spain/cala-macarelleta.htm

Basque Country

Barinatxe - La Salvaje Beach
Sopela / Biscay
https://www.inspain.org/en/vizcaya/getxo/beaches/barinatxe-la-salvaje/

Muriel Beach
Barrika
https://www.inspain.org/en/vizcaya/barrika/beaches/muriola/

Playa Nudista Ondarroa / Siete Playas
Gipuzkoa
https://www.beachrex.com/en/spain/pais-vasco/mutriku-beaches/playa-nudista-ondarroa

Canary Islands

See **AFRICA.**

Catalonia

Cala de Home Mort Stiges
Stiges (outskirts)
https://www.beachatlas.com/platja-de-lhome-mort

La Musclera Beach
Arenys de Mar
https://www.inspain.org/en/barcelona/arenys-de-mar/beaches/la-musclera/

Mar Bella Beach
Barcelona
https://barcelonando.com/marbella-beach/

Playa de las Balmins

Stiges
https://www.sitgesanytime.com/en/pl96/explore/beaches-and-
    ports/beaches/id2/balmins.htm

Playa de la Bassa Rodona
Sitges
https://www.worldbeachguide.com/spain/platja-de-la-bassa-
rodona.htm

El Torn Beach
Vandellòs i l'Hospitalet de l'Infant
https://www.inspain.org/en/tarragona/vandellos-i-lhospitalet-
de-linfant/beaches/el-torn/

Cantabria

Covachos Beach
Santa Cruz de Bezana
https://www.inspain.org/en/cantabria/santa-cruz-de-bezana/
beaches/covachos/

Community of Madrid

El Parque de Casa de Campo
Madrid
https://www.wheretoqueer.com/places/gay-nudist-area-in-el-
parque-de-casa-de-campo-in-madrid

Pantano de San Juan
Madrid / San Martin de Valdeiglesias
https://www.wheretoqueer.com/places/playa-nudiste-pantano-
de-san-juan

Costa Brava

Cala Estreta
Catalonia
https://nudistcompass.com/place/535

Cala del Senyor Ramon

Santa Cristina d'Aro
https://costabrava.org/en/what-to-do/beaches-and-coves/cala-del-senyor-ramon/

Cala Jugadora
Cadaqués
https://www.timeout.com/girona/things-to-do/cala-jugadora

Cala Tavallera
Cap de Creus
https://www.timeout.com/girona/things-to-do/cala-tavallera

L'lla Roja
Begur
https://www.timeout.com/barcelona/outdoor/platja-illa-roja

Cala Vallpresona
Tossa de Mar
https://www.timeout.com/girona/things-to-do/cala-vallpresona

Platja de Castell
Palamós
https://www.visitacostabrava.com/en/palamos/what-to-visit/
    beaches-and-coves/platja-del-castell

Galicia

Combouzas Beach
Arteixo
https://www.worldbeachguide.com/spain/praia-das-combouzas.htm

Valencia

Cala del Ambolo
Benitachell
https://www.worldbeachguide.com/spain/cala-del-ambolo.htm

SWEDEN

OUTDOORS:

Ågesta Beach
Stockholm / Farsta
https://www.scandinavianaturist.org/EOS/en/node/69

Amundön
Göteborg
https://www.scandinavianaturist.org/sv/node/130

Ältaren
Malmköping
https://www.scandinavianaturist.org/en/node/113

Ängelholm
Ängelholm
https://www.scandinavianaturist.org/en/node/113

Ängsö
Västerås / Enköping
https://www.scandinavianaturist.org/en/node/108

Ålabodarna
Landskrona
https://www.scandinavianaturist.org/en/node/175

Ardre
Gotland
https://www.scandinavianaturist.org/sv/node/352

Brunnsviken

Nationalstadsparken, the National City Park, Stockholm
https://www.scandinavianaturist.org/en/node/119

Bjuggöbadet
Hycklinge
https://www.scandinavianaturist.org/sv/node/138

Björnö
Björkvik
https://www.scandinavianaturist.org/sv/node/117

Breviksbadet
Åkersberga
https://www.scandinavianaturist.org/sv/node/120

Dragonudden
Umeå
https://www.scandinavianaturist.org/sv/node/94

Fönebo at Norra Dellen
Hudiksvall
https://www.scandinavianaturist.org/en/node/89

Getterön
Varberg
https://www.scandinavianaturist.org/en/node/144

Gränsö
Västervik
https://www.scandinavianaturist.org/en/node/137

Gustavsberg
Nora
https://www.scandinavianaturist.org/en/node/111

Heden
Halmstad
https://www.scandinavianaturist.org/en/node/111

Herrfallet

Arboga
https://www.scandinavianaturist.org/en/node/110

Hökafältet
Mellbystrand/Laholm
https://www.scandinavianaturist.org/en/node/145

Hölick
Hudiksvall
https://www.scandinavianaturist.org/en/node/98

Källtorp
Stockholm
https://www.scandinavianaturist.org/en/node/123

Kalven Särö
Göteborg
https://www.scandinavianaturist.org/sv/node/134

Kärsön
Kärsön Island (north end)
Stockholm
https://www.scandinavianaturist.org/en/node/127

Kattholmen
Strömstad
https://www.scandinavianaturist.org/en/node/133

Killingsand
Robertsfors
https://www.scandinavianaturist.org/en/node/270

Knähaken
Helsingborg
https://www.scandinavianaturist.org/en/node/151

Kråkviken
Karlstad
https://www.scandinavianaturist.org/en/node/339

Lövnäsbadet
Stockholm
https://www.scandinavianaturist.org/sv/node/125

Lilla Älgsjön
Kolmården
https://www.scandinavianaturist.org/en/node/218

Lulviksbadet
Luleå
https://www.scandinavianaturist.org/en/node/88

Lyckesand
Böda / Öland
https://www.scandinavianaturist.org/en/node/147

Lynga
Halmstad
https://www.scandinavianaturist.org/en/node/143

Långaveka
Falkenberg
https://www.scandinavianaturist.org/en/node/146

Malsjön
Åker
https://www.scandinavianaturist.org/en/node/109

Malmön
Sotenäs
https://www.scandinavianaturist.org/en/node/379

Mollön Peninsula Beach
Mollön Peninsula (southwest), Uddevalla
https://www.scandinavianaturist.org/en/node/132

Norsta Auren
Fårö / Gotland

https://www.scandinavianaturist.org/en/node/230

Pene
Växjö
https://www.scandinavianaturist.org/en/node/332

PGs Udde
Stockholm
https://www.scandinavianaturist.org/en/node/126#:~:text=PGs
Udde is a rocky,min walk along the lake.

Pite Ocean Beach
Piteå
https://www.scandinavianaturist.org/en/node/90

Östabadet
Tärnsjö
https://www.scandinavianaturist.org/en/node/101

Östra Holmen
Västerås
https://www.scandinavianaturist.org/en/node/112

Ribersborgsbadet
Malmö
https://www.scandinavianaturist.org/en/node/150

Rolstorpasjön
Vaggeryd
https://www.scandinavianaturist.org/en/node/292

Rullsand
Gävle
https://www.scandinavianaturist.org/en/node/99

Säby Träsk Nude Beach
Vaxholm
https://www.scandinavianaturist.org/en/node/128

Sandarne

Söderhamn
https://www.scandinavianaturist.org/en/node/272

Sandhammaren
Ystad
https://www.scandinavianaturist.org/en/node/171

Sandvikarna Vålön
Kristinehamn
https://www.scandinavianaturist.org/en/node/106

Sandviken
Filipstad
https://www.scandinavianaturist.org/en/node/107

Sandviken i Önskasjön
Örnsköldsvik
https://www.scandinavianaturist.org/en/node/93

Skibbiken Nude Beach
Sorsele
https://www.scandinavianaturist.org/en/node/91

Skutberget
Karlstad
https://www.scandinavianaturist.org/en/node/105

Skälsnäs Beach North
Växjö
https://www.scandinavianaturist.org/en/node/275

Smackgrundet
Timrå
https://www.scandinavianaturist.org/en/node/96

Smitska Udden Nude Beach
Göteborg
https://www.scandinavianaturist.org/en/node/135

Stamsjöbadet

Åsele
https://www.scandinavianaturist.org/en/node/92

Stora Hornsjön
Frillesås
https://www.scandinavianaturist.org/en/node/374

Storsand
Mjällom
https://www.scandinavianaturist.org/en/node/95

Svanrevet
Skanör
https://www.scandinavianaturist.org/en/node/149

Svärdsön
Saltsjöbaden/Stockholm
https://www.scandinavianaturist.org/sv/node/129

Tallparksbade
Öregrund
https://www.scandinavianaturist.org/en/node/103

Tjuvahålan
Halmstad
https://www.scandinavianaturist.org/en/node/142

Torpesand
Ingarö
https://www.scandinavianaturist.org/en/node/273

Trumöbadet
Mullhyttan/Örebro
https://www.scandinavianaturist.org/en/node/116

Truvebadet Nude Beach
Lidköping
https://www.scandinavianaturist.org/en/node/131

Tullan Nude Beach

Södertälje
https://www.scandinavianaturist.org/en/node/122

Tyge Backåkra
Ystad
https://www.scandinavianaturist.org/en/node/170

Viggebybadet
Linköping
https://www.scandinavianaturist.org/en/node/139

Värsnäs
Kalmar
https://www.scandinavianaturist.org/en/node/269

Vätterviksbadet
Vadstena / Motala
https://www.scandinavianaturist.org/en/node/136

Yngsjö
Kristianstad
https://www.scandinavianaturist.org/en/node/136

Ystad Strandskog
Ystad
https://www.scandinavianaturist.org/en/node/136

SWITZERLAND

WELLNESS:

Men Bodywork Workshop
Zürich
http://menbodywork.ch/

UNITED KINGDOM

LODGING:

Adam's Retreat
Moreton Pinkney
Banbury, England
https://www.adamsretreat.co.uk

Hamilton Hall
Dorset, England
https://www.hamiltonhall.info/about-hamilton-hall

Pride Lodge
Blackpool, England
https://www.pridelodge.com

OUTDOORS:

Black Rock Beach
Brighton, England
https://www.visitbrighton.com/things-to-do/brighton-naturist-beach-p628201

Botany Bay
Kent, England
Marine Dr, Broadstairs CT10 3LG, UK
https://www.thebeachguide.co.uk/south-east-england/kent/botany-bay.htm

Druridge Bay
Northumberland
Morpeth, England

https://www.thebeachguide.co.uk/north-east-england/
northumberland/druridge-bay.htm

Hampstead Heath

North London, England
https://www.cityoflondon.gov.uk/things-to-do/green-spaces/
hampstead-heath/where-to-go-at-hampstead-heath/highgate-
mens-pond

Holkham Bay

Norfolk, England
Norfolk Coast Path, King's Lynn PE31 8JJ
https://www.coolplaces.co.uk/places/uk/england/norfolk/1090-
holkham-bay

Pedn Vounder and Treen

Cornwall, England
S W Coast Path, St Levan, Penzance TR19 6LF, UK
https://www.cornwall-beaches.co.uk/west-cornwall/pedn-
vounder.htm

Rhossili Bay

Swansea, Wales
Rhossili, Swansea SA3 1PR, UK
https://www.thebeachguide.co.uk/south-wales/glamorgan/
rhossili-bay.htm

Rye Harbour Nature Reserve

East Sussex, England
Harbour Rd, Rye TN31 7TX, UK
https://www.walkingclub.org.uk/nudist-beach/Rye-Sussex.html

Studland Naturist Beach

Dorset, England
S W Coast Path BH19 3BA, UK
https://www.swanage.co.uk/naturist-beach/

Walney Island

Cumbria, Walney

Barrow-in-Furness LA14 3BP, UK
https://www.walkingclub.org.uk/nudist-beach/Walney-Island-Cumbria.html

Winterton Dunes Nature Reserve
Norfolk, England
Great Yarmouth NR29 4BJ, UK
https://www.visiteastofengland.com/attraction_activity/
    winterton-dunes-national-nature-reserve

Weston Mouth Beach
Devon, England
https://www.thebeachguide.co.uk/south-west-england/devon/
weston-mouth.htm

WELLNESS:

Brewster Street Yoga
London
https://www.brewerstreetyoga.com/mens-naked-yoga

Male London Socials
London
https://www.malelondonsocials.org.uk

NORTH AMERICA

CANADA

LODGING:

Domaine Emeraude
Montreal, Quebec
http://www.domaine-emeraude.com/community.htm

The Point Resort
Vittoria, Ontario
https://get-tothepoint.com

Riverside RV Campground
Tweed, Ontario
https://www.riversidervcampground.com

OUTDOORS:

Beaconia Beach
Winnepeg, Manitoba
https://beaconiabeach.ca/

Blooming Point Beach
Charlottetown, Prince Edward Island
https://pointseastcoastaldrive.com/things-to-do/entry/
blooming-point-beach

Crystal Crescent Beach
Halifax, Nova Scotia
http://www.bluenosenaturists.com/the-beach/

Hanlan's Point
Toronto, Ontario
https://www.torontoisland.com/hanlans.php

Oka National Park
Oka, Quebec
https://mtltimes.ca/life/oka-beach-clothing-is-optional/

Paradise Beach
Saskatoon, Saskatchewan
https://beachnearby.com/en-US/beach/paradise-beach-saskatoon

Wreck Beach
Vancouver, BC
https://vancouversbestplaces.com/top-attractions/vancouvers-best-beaches/wreck-beach/

COSTA RICA

LODGING:

The XT 10
Ojochal
https://thext10.com

OUTDOORS:

Club Mi Amor (beach)
Puerto Viejo Cahuita, Manzanillo
https://hostal-riopalmas-club-mi-amor.negocio.site/

Manuel Antonio Beach - Playa Playita
Manuel Antonio National Park & Quepos,Puntarenas Province, Quepos
https://www.costarica.com/attractions/playitas-beach

Montezuma Beach
Puntarenas Province, Santa Fe, Costa Rica
https://montezuma-costarica.com/

MEXICO

LODGING:

Piñata
Puerto Vallarta, Jalisco
https://www.pinatapv.com

Salty Boys
https://saltyboys.com/

OUTDOORS:

Casa Cuppula Pool Club
Puerto Vallarta, Jalisco
https://www.casacupula.com/pool-club/

Jet's Naked Boat Tour
Puerto Vallarta, Jalisco
https://www.jetsprivateboattours.com/boat-tours/naked/

Playa del Amor
Playa del Carmen
https://www.google.com/maps/place/Playa+Del+Amor/
@20.5912556,-87.0939447,15.37z/data=!4m14!1m7!3m6!
1s0x8f4e436850efa2a7:0x94d1ec010d8cb66a!2sPlaya+Del
+Amor!8m2!3d20.5942756!4d-87.0983095!16s/g/11rxpfqywj!
3m5!1s0x8f4e436850efa2a7:0x94d1ec010d8cb66a!8m2!
3d20.5942756!4d-87.0983095!16s/g/11rxpfqywj?entry=ttu

Playa del Amor
San Pedro Pochutla
https://www.worldbeachguide.com/mexico/playa-del-

amor-1.htm

Playa Zipolite
San Pedro Pochutla, Oaxaca
https://www.worldbeachguide.com/mexico/playa-zipolite.htm

WELLNESS:

Spartacus Sauna for Men
Puerto Vallarta, Jalisco
http://www.spaspartacus.com/store/c1/Featured_Products.html

UNITED STATES

Arizona

LODGING:

Arizona Sunburst Inn
Pheonix
https://www.azsunburst.com

Copper Cactus Ranch
Queen Valley
https://www.coppercactusranch.com

Happy Endings Retreat
Morristown
http://www.happyendingsretreat.com/

Tony's House
Pheonix
https://tonycabralre.com/

OUTDOORS:

Tanque Verde Falls
Tucson
https://www.tucsontopia.com/tanque-verde-falls/

WELLNESS:

Arizona Nude Games
Pheonix
https://aznudegames.org

Bear Naked Yoga
Pheonix
https://www.bearnakedyogi.com

Arkansas

WELLNESS:

Buckstaff Bathhouse
Hot Springs
https://www.buckstaffbaths.com

California

Los Angeles

WELLNESS:

Century Day & Night Spa
Los Angeles
https://centurydayandnightspa.com

M.E.N. Yoga & Fitness
West Hollywood
https://www.menyoga.club

Naked Warrior Yoga
West Hollywood
https://www.nakedwarrioryoga.com

Palm Springs

LODGING:

All Worlds
Central Palm Springs
https://www.allworlds.com

Canyon Club
North Palm Springs
https://www.canyonclubhotel.com/

CCBC
Cathedral City
https://www.ccbcresorthotel.com

Descanso
North Palm Springs
https://descansoresort.com

Desert Paradise Resort
Central Palm Springs
https://www.desertparadise.com

El Mirasol Villas Resort
Central Palm Springs
https://www.elmirasol.com

The Hacienda at Warm Sands
Central Palm Springs
https://thehacienda.com

Inndulge
Central Palm Springs
https://inndulge.com

Santiago
South Palm Springs
https://santiagoresort.com

Triangle Inn Palm Springs
South Palm Springs
https://www.triangle-inn.com

Twin Palms
South Palm Springs
https://twinpalmsresort.com

Vista Grande
Central Plam Springs
https://www.vistagranderesort.com

OUTDOORS:

Red Rock Trees at Whitewater
Whitewater Preserve
-just south of the cement bridge over the creek
https://wildlandsconservancy.org/preserves/whitewater

WELLNESS:

Desert Springs Spa at the JW Marriott Palm Desert
Palm Desert
https://www.desertspringsspa.com/

Naked Yoga with Denny At the Triangle Inn
Palm Springs
https://www.triangle-inn.com

Spa Night at Men's Grooming Spot
Cathedral City
2nd & 4th Tuesday, 7:30 to 11:00 P.M.
https://mensgroomingspot.com/

The Spa at Séc-he
Palm Springs
https://thespaatseche.com/

Sunstone Spa at Agua Caliente Casino Ranch Mirage
Rancho Mirage
https://www.desertspringsspa.com/

San Diego

OUTDOORS:

Black's Beach
La Jolla
https://www.californiabeaches.com/beach/blacks-beach-san-diego/

San Onofre State Beach

South Orange County - Camp Pendleton
https://www.californiabeaches.com/beach/san-onofre-state-beach-nude-area/

WELLNESS:

Aqua Day Spa
Kearny-Mesa
http://aquadayspasd.com

San Diego Naked Yoga
San Diego
https://sdnakedyoga.square.site

Yu Spa
Kearny-Mesa
https://yuspasd.com

San Francisco

LODGING:

Wildwood
Guerneville
https://www.wildwoodfoundation.org

The Woods @ Russian River
Guerneville
https://russianriverhotel.com

OUTDOORS:

Black Sands
Sausaito
https://www.californiabeaches.com/beach/black-sands-beach-marin-headlands/

Fort Funston
San Francisco
https://www.californiabeaches.com/beach/fort-funston-beach/

Gray Whale Cove
Montara
https://www.californiabeaches.com/beach/gray-whale-cove-state-beach/

Marshall's
San Francisco
https://www.californiabeaches.com/beach/marshall-beach/

North Baker
San Francisco
https://www.californiabeaches.com/beach/north-baker-beach/

Red Rock Beach
Stinson Beach
https://www.californiabeaches.com/beach/red-rock-beach/

San Gregorio Private
San Gregorio
https://www.californiabeaches.com/beach/san-gregorio-private-beach/

South Rodeo
Sausalito
https://www.californiabeaches.com/beach/south-rodeo-beach/

WELLNESS:

Imperial Spa
Japantown
http://stage.imperialdayspa.com

Kabuki Springs and Spa
Japantown
https://kabukisprings.com

Naked Yoga for Men
San Francisco
http://nakedyogasf.com

California - other cities

OUTDOORS:

More Mesa Beach
Santa Barbara
https://www.californiabeaches.com/beach/more-mesa-beach/

Pirate's Cove Beach
Avilla Beach
https://www.californiabeaches.com/beach/pirates-cove-beach-
avila-beach/

Secret Cove Beach
Lake Tahoe (Carson City, Nevada)
1.5 miles south of Sand Harbor
https://www.tahoepublicbeaches.org/beaches/secret-cove/

Colorado

OUTDOORS:

Valley View Hot Springs
Moffat
https://www.olt.org/vvhs

Conundrum Hot Springs
Snowmass/Aspen
https://www.recreation.gov/permits/273336

Strawberry Hot Springs
Steamboat Springs
https://strawberryhotsprings.com

Florida

Fort Lauderdale

LODGING:

The Augstin Men's Guesthouse

Fort Lauderdale
https://theagustin.com/

The Big Coconut
Fort Lauderdale
http://thebigcoconutguesthouse.com

Cabanas
Fort Lauderdale
https://thecabanasguesthouse.com

Calypso Inn
Fort Lauderdale
https://calypsoinnwiltonmanors.com

Casa Citron
Fort Lauderdale
https://www.casacitron.com

Cheston House
Fort Lauderdale
https://www.chestonhouse.com

Ed Lugo Resort
Fort Lauderdale
https://edlugoresort.com

Grand Resort
Fort Lauderdale
http://thegrandresortandspa.com

Inn Leather
Fort Lauderdale
https://www.innleather.com

 Pineapple Point
Fort Lauderdale
https://www.pineapplepoint.com/

Signature Florida Inns

Fort Lauderdale
https://www.signaturefloridaguesthouses.com

Worthington Resorts
Fort Lauderdale
https://theworthington.com

OUTDOORS:

Haulover Beach
Sunny Isles Beach (Miami/Fort Lauderdale)
https://www.miamidade.gov/parks/haulover.asp

WELLNESS:

Arco Iros Yoga
Fort Lauderdale
http://www.arcoirisyoga.com

Club Fort Lauderdale
Fort Lauderdale
https://www.clubftl.com

Key West

LODGING:

Equator Resort
Key West
https://equatorresort.com

Island House
Key West
https://islandhousekeywest.com/#group-6

New Orleans House
Key West
http://www.neworleanshousekw.com

OUTDOORS:

Anne's Beach

Islamorada, Matecunbe Key
https://floridakeystreasures.com/beaches/annesbeach/

Boca Chica Beach
Geiger Key
https://www.atlasobscura.com/places/geiger-key-abandoned-beach

Miami

OUTDOORS:

Haulover Beach
Sunny Isles Beach (Miami/Fort Lauderdale)
https://www.miamidade.gov/parks/haulover.asp

WELLNESS:

Club Aqua Miami
Miami
https://www.clubaquamiami.com

Naked Yoga Miami
Miami
http://nakedyogamiami.com

Tampa

LODGING:

Casa Del Merman
St. Petersburg
https://www.gaystpetehouse.com/

Casa Puente
Tampa
https://www.casapuentebnb.com/home

OUTDOORS:

Apollo Beach Nature Preserve
Apollo Beach

https://www.tripadvisor.com/ShowUserReviews-g29170-d9723450-r693926269-Apollo_Beach_Nature_Preserve-Apollo_Beach_Florida.html

Florida - other cities

LODGING:

Camp Mars
Venus
https://campmars.com/

Vitambi Springs Resort
Clewiston
https://vitambi.com

OUTDOORS:

Apollo Beach
New Smyrna Beach
https://www.nps.gov/cana/planyourvisit/hours.htm

Blind Creek Beach
Fort Pierce/ St. Lucie Inlet
https://www.treasurecoastnaturists.org

Bunche Beach
Fort Myers
https://www.leegov.com/parks/beaches/bunche

Cypress Cove Nudist Resort
Orlando
https://cypresscoveresort.com/

Hobe Sound Beach
Hobe Sound/ Juniper Island
https://discovermartin.com/directory/hobe-sound-beach/

Johnson's Beach
Pensacola
Perdido Key Area of Gulf Islands National Seashore

https://www.visitpensacola.com/directory/johnson-beach-gulf-islands-national-seashore/

Playalinda Beach
Titusville
Playalinda Beach Road, Canaveral National Seashore
https://floridahikes.com/playalinda-beach

Santa Rosa Beach
Destin
https://www.worldbeachguide.com/usa/santa-rosa-beach.htm

St. George State Park Beach
Eastpoint/ Tallahassee
https://www.worldbeachguide.com/usa/st-george-island.htm

Georgia

LODGING:

The Hideaway Campground
Collins
https://royshideaway.com/about-us/

In the Woods
Canon
https://inthewoodscampground.com

OZ Campground and Resort
Unadilla
https://www.ozcampground.com/

The River's Edge
Dewey Rose
https://camptheriversedge.com

WELLNESS:

Jeju Sauna & Spa Home of Wellbeing
Duluth

https://jejusauna.com

Hawai'i

LODGING:

Isle of You
Puna, Hawai'i
http://www.isleofyounaturally.com

OUTDOORS:

Beach 69
Kona, Hawai'i
Old Puako Rd, Waimea, HI 96743
https://dlnr.hawaii.gov/dar/marine-managed-areas/hawaii-marine-life-conservation-districts/hawaii-waialea-bay/

Kahena Beach
Puna, Hawai'i
Kalapana-Kapoho Road, Pohoa
https://thishawaiilife.com/kehena-beach/

Little Beach
Mekena State Beach. Maui
https://dlnr.hawaii.gov/dsp/parks/maui/makena-state-park/

Polo Beach
Waialua, Oahu
68-1009 Farrington Hwy
https://exposetonature.org/HI/polo-beach

Idaho

OUTDOORS:

Jerry Johnson Hot Springs
Clearwater National Forest
https://www.fs.usda.gov/recarea/nezperceclearwater/recarea/?recid=80549

Illinois

LODGING:

The Den Off Eastlake
Chicago
https://www.thedenoffeastlake.com/

WELLNESS:

Chicago Sweatlodge
Chicago
https://chicago-sweatlodge.business.site/

King Spa
Chicago/ Niles, Illinois
https://www.kingspa.com/chicago/

Windy City Naked Yoga
Chicago
https://www.meetup.com/windy-city-naked-yoga/

Indiana

LODGING:

Camp Buckwood
Morgantown
https://campbuckwood.com

WELLNESS:

Club Indianapolis
Indiana
http://www.clubsaunas.com/club_indianapolis/

Iowa

OUTDOORS:

Bare Butt Hill Beach
North Liberty

https://www.gayoutdoors.org/page.cfm?typeofsite=directory-detail&id=524

Kentucky

LODGING:

River Ridge Campground & RV Park
Mount Olivet
https://www.riverridgecampground.com

Maine

LODGING:

Twin Ponds Lodge
Albion
https://www.twinpondslodge.com

OUTDOORS:

Frenchmen's Hole (lower pool)
Newry
https://seeswim.com/location/frenchmans-hole/

Massachusetts

LODGING:

Crew's Quarters Provincetown
Provincetown (hotel not nude, but has a nude sun deck)
https://www.crewsquartersptown.com

OUTDOORS:

Herring Cove Beach
Provincetown
https://www.nps.gov/caco/planyourvisit/herring-cove-beach.htm

Moshup Beach
Martha's Vineyard

https://www.savebuzzardsbay.org/places-to-go/moshup-beach/

Michigan

LODGING:

CreekRidge Campground
Stockbridge
https://creekridgecampground.com

Camp Boomerang
Woodward
https://michigangaycamping.com/

OUTDOORS:

Saugatuck Oval Beach
Saugatuck
https://gaysaugatuckdouglas.com/saugatuck-oval-beach/

Mississippi

OUTDOORS:

West Ship Island Beach
Biloxi, Harrison County
https://www.nudeplaces.de/united-states/west-ship-island_biloxi-harrison-county

Missouri

LODGING:

Cactus Canyon Campground & Resort
Ozarks / Ava
http://www.cactuscanyoncampground.com
WELLNESS:

Club ST. Louis
St. Louis
http://www.clubsaunas.com/club_st_louis/

Nevada

OUTDOORS:

Secret Cove Beach - Lake Tahoe
Carson City
1.5 miles south of Sand Harbor
https://www.tahoepublicbeaches.org/beaches/secret-cove/

WELLNESS:

Qua Baths & Spa (Caesar's Palace)
Las Vegas
https://www.caesars.com/caesars-palace/things-to-do/qua

Spa Mandalay (Mandalay Bay)
Las Vegas
https://mandalaybay.mgmresorts.com/en/amenities/spas.html

New Hampshire

LODGING:

Joe's Hideaway Campground
Washington
https://joeshideaway.com

New Jersey

OUTDOORS:

Gunnison Beach
Sandy Hook
Gunnison Beach, Atlantic Dr, Highlands, NJ 07732
https://www.nps.gov/places/000/sandy-hook-beach-g-gunnison-beach.htm

New Mexico

OUTDOORS:

Black Rock Hot Springs
Taos
https://blackrockdesert.org/explore-black-rock/hot-springs/

Gila Hot Springs (clothing optional after dark)
Siver Springs
http://gilahotspringscampground.com/

Manby Hot Springs
Taos / Arroyo Hondo
https://www.ultimatehotspringsguide.com/manby-hot-springs.html

Montezuma Hot Springs
Las Vegas
https://www.ultimatehotspringsguide.com/8203montezuma-hot-springs.html

Ponce de Leon Hot Springs
Taos / Carson National Forest
https://www.ultimatehotspringsguide.com/ponce-de-leon-hot-springs.html

San Antonio Hot Springs
Jemez
https://www.ultimatehotspringsguide.com/8203san-antonio-hot-springs.html

Spence Hot Springs
Jemez
https://www.fs.usda.gov/recarea/santafe/recarea/?recid=75826

WELLNESS:

Blackstone Hot Springs and Lodging
Truth or Consequences
https://www.blackstonehotsprings.com/

Indian Springs Bathhouse

Truth or Consequences
https://www.blackstonehotsprings.com/hotspring-baths/

New York

LODGING:

Belvedere Guesthouse
Fire Island
https://www.belvederefireisland.com/welcome

Easton Mountain
Greenwich
https://www.eastonmountain.org/

Jones Pond Campground
Angelica
https://www.jonespond.com

OUTDOORS:

Cherry Grove Beach
Lewis Walk, Fire Island
https://fireisland.com/towns/cherry-grove-fire-island/

Gunnison Beach
Sandy Hook, New Jersey
Gunnison Beach, Atlantic Dr, Highlands, NJ 07732
https://www.nps.gov/places/000/sandy-hook-beach-g-gunnison-beach.htm

Kismet Nude Beach
Cedar Street, Fire Island
https://fireisland.com/beaches/kismet-beach-fire-island/

The Pines Beach
Bay Walk, Fire Island
https://fireisland.com/towns/fire-island-pines-fire-island/

WELLNESS:

Growl NYC Yoga - NYC
New York City
https://www.meetup.com/growlnyc/

MMX Massage and Yoga - NYC
New York City
Private club, apply before you go.
https://www.mmxnyc.com

Russian Baths of New York - NYC
New York City
http://russianbathofny.com

Russian & Turkish Baths - NYC
New York City
https://www.russianturkishbaths.com

North Carolina

OUTDOORS:

Ocracoke Ramp 67
Ocracoke Island
https://www.nps.gov/places/000/beach-access-ramp-67.htm

Ohio

LODGING:

Circle JJ Ranch Campground
Scio
https://circlejjranch.com

Freedom Valley Campground
New London
https://freedomvalleycamping.com

WELLNESS:

Club Columbus
Columbus

http://www.clubsaunas.com/club_columbus/

Oregon

LODGING:

Bamboo Acres
Talent
https://bambooacres.org/

OUTDOORS:

Collins Beach
Portland
https://sauvieisland.org/visitor-information/public-beaches/

Rooster Rock State Beach
Portland
https://stateparks.oregon.gov/index.cfm?
do=park.profile&parkId=126

WELLNESS:

Sunray Yoga
Portland
https://www.sunray-yoga.com/

Pennsylvania

LODGING:

The Woods Campground
Lehighton
https://www.thewoodscampground.com

Rhode Island

OUTDOORS:

Mohegan Bluffs Beach
Block Island
https://www.blockislandinfo.com/island-events/mohegan-

bluffs

Tennessee

LODGING:

My Whispering Oaks
Hampshire
https://mywhisperingoaks.org

Texas

LODGING:

Circle J Guest Ranch:
(See calendar for men's events.)
Eustace
https://circlejguestranch.com/

Grizzly Pines
Navasota
https://www.grizzlypines.com/

OUTDOORS:

Barton Springs Pool Beach - Sandy Beach
Austin
https://beachcatcher.com/beach/barton-springs-pool-beach

Emerald Lake Naturist Resort and RV Park Beach
Porter
https://www.emeraldlakeresorthouston.com/index.html

Hippie Hallow at Lake Travis
Austin
https://parks.traviscountytx.gov/parks/hippie-hollow

McFaddin Beach
Port Arthur/ Bolivar Peninsula
https://visitportarthurtx.com/things-to-do/attraction/
mcfaddin-beach/

Padre Island National Seashore
Padre Island
Padre Island https://www.nps.gov/pais/index.htm

UFO Beach
South Padre Island
https://beachcatcher.com/beach/ufo-beach

WELLNESS:

Austin Naked Yoga
Austi
https://www.austinnakedyoga.com/y

Club Dallas
Dallas
Dallashttp://www.clubsaunas.com/club_dallas/

Club Houston
Houston
https://www.club-houston.com/

Naked Yoga Camp
Austin
https://www.nakedyogacamp.com/

San Antonio Naked Yoga
San Antonio
http://www.sanantonionakedyoga.com

Utah

OUTDOORS:

Diamond Fork Hot Springs
Spanish Fork
https://www.fs.usda.gov/recarea/uwcnf/recarea/?recid=9861

Vermont

LODGING:

Frog Meadow Resort
Newfane
https://www.frogmeadow.com/gay-bed-and-breakfast-resort-new-england/

The Gargoyle House
Newbury
https://www.gargoylehouse.com/english/homepage.php

OUTDOORS:

The Punchbowl
Waitsfield
https://maps.roadtrippers.com/us/waitsfield-vt/nature/the-punchbowl-skinnydipping

Virginia

WELLNESS:

Spa World
Centreville
https://spaworldusa.com

West Virginia

LODGING:

Rosalind Resort & Campground
Proctor
https://www.roselandwv.com

Washington

OUTDOORS:

Denny Blaine Beach
Seattle
https://www.seattle.gov/parks/find/parks/denny-blaine-park

Howell Park
Seattle
https://www.seattle.gov/parks/find/parks/howell-park

WELLNESS:
Powers of Man
Seattle
https://www.powersofman.com/

SOUTH AMERICA

BRAZIL

LODGING:

Gay Nude Sail
https://gaysail.com/

OUTDOORS:

Abrico Beach
Rio de Janeiro
https://www.worldbeachguide.com/brazil/praia-abrico.htm

Massarandupió Beach
Entre Rios
https://www.worldbeachguide.com/brazil/massarandupio.htm

Olho de Boi Beach
Búzios
https://www.worldbeachguide.com/brazil/olho-de-boi.htm

Praia Brava - Cabo Frio
Cabo Frio
https://www.worldbeachguide.com/brazil/praia-brava.htm

Praia Brava - Trindade
Parati
https://www.worldbeachguide.com/brazil/praia-brava-trindade.htm

Praia da Galheta
Florianópolis
https://www.worldbeachguide.com/brazil/praia-galheta.htm

Praia de Grumari
Rio de Janeiro
https://www.worldbeachguide.com/brazil/praia-abrico.htm

Praia do Pinho
Balneário Camboriú
https://www.worldbeachguide.com/brazil/praia-do-pinho.htm

Tambaba Beach
Pitimbu
https://www.worldbeachguide.com/brazil/tambaba.htm

URAGUAY

LODGING:

Undaris
Maldonado
https://www.undarius.com

OUTDOORS:

Chihuahua Beach
Portozuelo Bay
Punta del Este - outskirts
https://worldbeachlist.com/Explore/Uruguay/Maldonado/
Maldonado/Playa-Chihuahua

Printed in Great Britain
by Amazon

41479126R00076